LOOK INSIDE

AN EGYPTIAN TOMB

BRIAN MOSES
Illustrated by Adam Hook

Editor: Jason Hook
Series design: Ian Winton
Book design: Heather Blackham
Cover designer: Rachel Hamdi

First published in 1997 by Wayland Publishers Ltd,
This edition published in 2001 by Hodder Wayland
An imprint of Hodder Children's Books
This edition published in 2007 by Wayland,
an imprint of Hachette Children's Books
338 Euston Road
London NW1 3BH

© Wayland 1997

British Library Cataloguing in Publication Data
Moses, Brian, 1950-
Look inside an Egyptian Tomb
1. Tombs – Egypt – Juvenile literature 2. Egypt – Social
life and customs – To 332 BC. – Juvenile literature
I.Title II.Hook, Adam III.An Egyptian tomb
932
ISBN 978 0 7502 5204 1

Printed and bound in China

Picture Acknowledgements
The publishers would like to thank the following for permission
to reproduce their pictures: (t=top; c=centre; b=bottom; l=left;
r=right) AKG 22t, 25c; Axiom *cover* c, 4, 5t, 6, 7t, 7c, 8t, 9c,
9b, 12t, 16b, 17, 18br, 19r, 23t, 25b, 26l; British Museum *cover*
l, 11b, 18bl, 19l, 28b, 29; Werner Forman Archive *cover* r, 8b,
9t, 12c, 12b, 13t, 14, 15c, 16t, 18t, 20, 24t, 26r, 28t; Robert
Harding *cover* t, 10, 11t, 13b, 15t, 15b, 21t, 21br, 22b, 23b,
24b, 25t, 27l, 30; Pictor 5b, 7b, 21bl.

'In memory of my father, Harry Moses, who loved to
read about ancient lands and who first showed me the
mummies in the British Museum.' Brian Moses

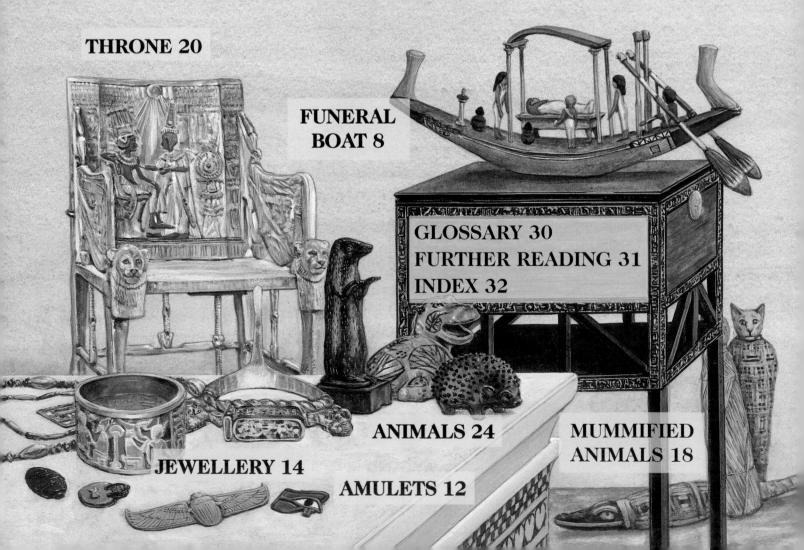

CONTENTS

TOMB

PREPARING FOR DEATH

Look inside an Egyptian tomb. On its cold, stone walls is a painting of Osiris, God of the Underworld. According to myth, Osiris was once king of Egypt. He was murdered by his jealous brother, but was reborn as a god. The Egyptian king, or Pharaoh, believes that he too will become a god when he dies. When he is crowned, he orders the royal architect to build him a magnificent tomb. It will guard the Pharaoh's body after his death, when his soul travels to join Osiris.

▶ A tomb painting of Osiris, who gave the Pharaoh hope of everlasting life.

'Time laughs at all things, but the pyramids laugh at time.'[1]

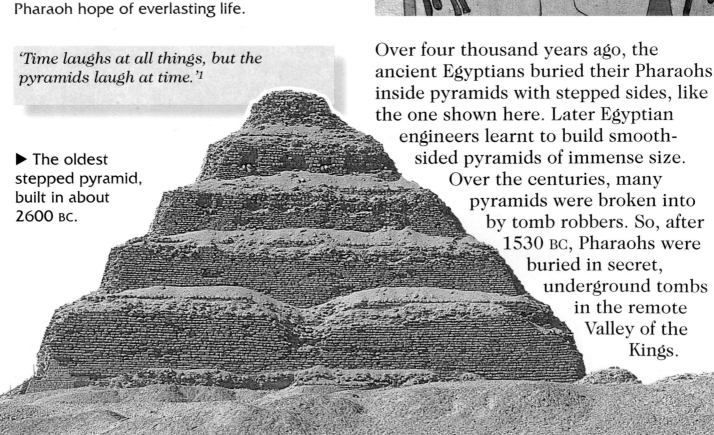

▶ The oldest stepped pyramid, built in about 2600 BC.

Over four thousand years ago, the ancient Egyptians buried their Pharaohs inside pyramids with stepped sides, like the one shown here. Later Egyptian engineers learnt to build smooth-sided pyramids of immense size. Over the centuries, many pyramids were broken into by tomb robbers. So, after 1530 BC, Pharaohs were buried in secret, underground tombs in the remote Valley of the Kings.

◀ A magnificent temple built for a Pharaoh's queen.

The scroll, above, contains words from the Egyptian *Book of the Dead*. This was written on papyrus and left in the tomb. It contained magic spells to transform the Pharaoh into different animals, and passwords to guide his soul through the dangers of the Underworld.

▼ The Great Pyramid at Giza, tomb of King Cheops who ruled for 23 years until 2556 BC.

BURIAL CHAMBER

BUILDING THE TOMB

The newly crowned Pharaoh arrives in the Valley of the Kings, to inspect the building of his tomb. Porters emerge from the cliff-face carrying wicker baskets of broken stone. At the end of a sloping, candle-lit tunnel, stonemasons are chiselling the burial chamber ever deeper into the rock. The walls are being smoothed with plaster, and decorated with strange symbols by the finest painters in all of Egypt.

▶ A tomb painting of Egyptian builders at work.

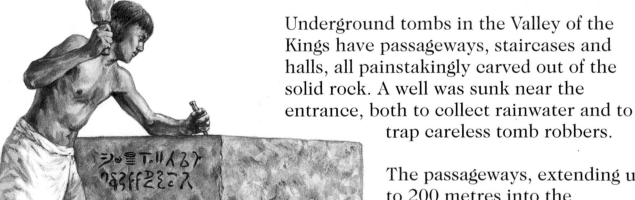

Underground tombs in the Valley of the Kings have passageways, staircases and halls, all painstakingly carved out of the solid rock. A well was sunk near the entrance, both to collect rainwater and to trap careless tomb robbers.

The passageways, extending up to 200 metres into the mountainside, are painted with scenes of the journey to the afterlife. Deep in the hillside is the Pharaoh's final resting place, the Hall of Gold.

◀ A stonemason cutting a block for a pyramid.

◀ Look inside the tomb of Pharaoh Rameses II.

The lion-faced god lays the foundations of your house.

▼ A gallery in the Great Pyramid.

Building a pyramid tomb was an even greater task, showing the amazing skills of the Egyptians. Astronomers made sure that the Great Pyramid's corners faced exactly to the four points of the compass. Labourers used ramps, ropes and levers to raise over two million blocks, weighing over two tonnes each, into a perfect pyramid.

As the pyramid rose, gaps were left for galleries, air shafts and sometimes a false burial hall. The finished pyramid was covered in dazzling, white limestone and a cap of gold. Within this magnificent mountain of stone was hidden the Pharaoh's burial chamber.

▶ The Great Pyramid is 146m high, taller than St Paul's Cathedral.

FUNERAL BOAT

RIVER JOURNEY

Hearing news of the young Pharaoh's death, the court has seventy days to prepare for his burial. His coffin is loaded aboard a barge of cedar, with a curved prow and stern and a canopy to shade the priest who accompanies the body. With a large steering oar, a boatman guides the funeral barge out into the River Nile.

▶ A funeral boat, pictured in a tomb in the Valley of the Kings.

People normally only lived to about thirty in Egyptian times. Tutankhamun, the Pharaoh whose treasure-filled tomb was unearthed by Howard Carter in 1922, was eighteen when he died. Model boats were placed in tombs to represent the river journey of the dead. They also symbolized the boat of the sun god Ra, who was believed to sail over the Earth each day carrying the sun. Tutankhamun's tomb contained a model boat made of alabaster, with ibex heads at each end.

◀ A model sailing boat.

Homage to thee, O Ra ... You sail over the heights of heaven and your heart is glad. Your Morning Boat meets your Evening Boat with fair winds.

◀ The reconstructed funeral barge of King Cheops.

The historian Herodotus wrote that, 'Egypt is the gift of the Nile.' The River Nile was the Egyptians' main highway, and many tomb paintings show boats carrying the enormous blocks of stone needed to build the pyramids. Full-size boats were sometimes buried in tombs, such as the 43-metre-long barge found beside the Great Pyramid.

▲ This model boat was raised up on wheels.

The River Nile enabled the Egyptians to survive. Perfect farming land was created in the middle of the desert, when the Nile flooded each year and left behind a layer of mud. This annual renewal of the land was a symbol of the dead Pharaoh's own rebirth.

◀ A tomb painting of a crocodile-god guiding the Pharaoh's soul.

9

CANOPIC JARS

REMOVING THE ORGANS

A procession carries the Pharaoh's body into the embalming workshop, called the Divine Hall of Anubis. Anubis is the god of mummification, who brought Osiris back to life. Priests chant sacred texts as the gruesome work begins. The body is washed and shaved. The chief embalmer inserts a hook into the Pharaoh's nose, and begins the removal of the brain.

▶ The embalmer prepares to remove the Pharaoh's brain.

The 'embalming' of the Pharaoh's body was the special process that protected it from decay. After the removal of the brain, a cut was made in the left side of the corpse. The embalmer then groped around inside to find the lungs, liver, stomach and intestines, and cut them out. The heart was left in place. It would be needed by the Pharaoh for the Weighing of the Heart, the ceremony in the Underworld that decided the fate of his soul or spirit.

> 'As much as possible of the brain is extracted through the nostrils with an iron hook, and what the hook cannot reach is rinsed out with drugs; next the flank is laid open with a flint knife and the whole contents of the abdomen removed.'[2]

◀ This jar from Tutankhamun's tomb held a perfume called 'unguent'.

The body was dried by packing it with a type of salt called natron. It was then left for forty days, before being stuffed with linen, sawdust, sand and clay; and perfumed with wine and sweet-smelling spices. Sometimes, the corpse was given glass eyes!

◄ A tomb painting showing Osiris and two canopic jars.

After removal, the vital organs were dried, wrapped in linen and stored in special containers called canopic jars. These jars had stoppers shaped in the forms of the sons of Horus, god of the rising sun. The jar containing the intestines had a falcon's head, the stomach a jackal, the lungs a baboon and the liver a human. The canopic jars were placed in the tomb in a wooden chest at the foot of the Pharaoh's sarcophagus.

◄ Canopic jars, showing gods in the forms of the falcon, jackal, baboon and human.

AMULETS

WRAPPING THE MUMMY

Embalmers now transform the Pharaoh into a mummy. They wrap his dried body in a red sheet and bind his head with linen. His fingers and toes are sheathed in gold. The embalmers wind layer after layer of bandages round his limbs, and bind his legs together. Finally, they wrap a wide bandage around the mummy's entire body.

▶ This tomb painting shows Anubis embalming Osiris, the first mummy.

▼ Amulets made from cowrie shells.

Bandaging the mummy took up to fifteen days. Each layer was sealed with resin. Lucky charms called amulets, of great value, were placed between the wrappings and inscribed with spells from the *Book of the Dead*. Tutankhamun's bandages contained 143 amulets. Occasionally, a careless embalmer also wrapped flies, lizards and even a mouse into the mummy's binding!

This spell was written on papyrus to protect a child:

'I have made ready for its protection a potion from the poisonous afat herb, from garlic which is bad for you, from honey which is sweet for the living but bitter for the dead, from the droppings and entrails of fish and beast and from the spine of the perch.'[3]

▶ This glass fragment shows the Pharaoh's magical 'was' sceptre in the shape of a swan's head.

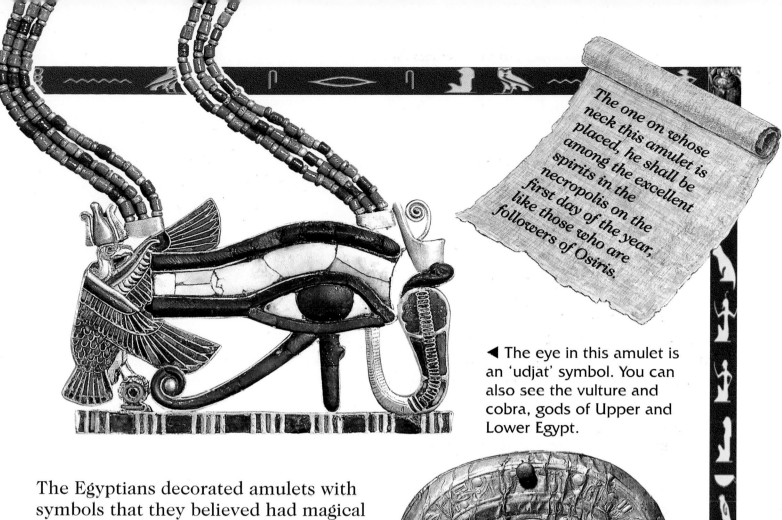

◄ The eye in this amulet is an 'udjat' symbol. You can also see the vulture and cobra, gods of Upper and Lower Egypt.

The Egyptians decorated amulets with symbols that they believed had magical powers. They wore them to keep away evil, bring good luck and increase fertility. Many amulets were grouped around the mummy's heart, as this was the part of the body the Egyptians associated with the spirit.

The *udjat,* or Eye of Horus, was a magic symbol that asked the god Horus to watch over you. It was placed on seals over the tomb doors, and on the flesh where the embalmer had cut into the mummy's side. The *ankh* was the Egyptian symbol of everlasting life, and was one of the hieroglyphics used to write the name of Tutankhamun. The Pharaoh's sceptre was in the shape of the magical *was* symbol.

▶ A gold mirror case shaped like an 'ankh' symbol.

JEWELLERY

PUTTING ON THE MASK

The embalmer puts on a mask shaped like a jackal's head, to make himself look like Anubis, god of mummification. Mumbling strange spells, he presses a magnificent gold 'death mask' over the mummy's bandaged face. This golden mask looks like the face of the dead Pharaoh. When the Pharaoh's spirit returns to the tomb, it will now be able to recognize its own mummified body.

▶ A priest dressed as Anubis prepares the mummy's mask.

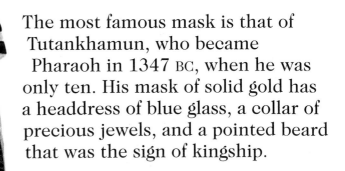

◀ The death mask of Tutankhamun, found in his tomb in the Valley of the Kings.

The most famous mask is that of Tutankhamun, who became Pharaoh in 1347 BC, when he was only ten. His mask of solid gold has a headdress of blue glass, a collar of precious jewels, and a pointed beard that was the sign of kingship.

Look inside an Egyptian tomb, and you will see a fabulous display of jewellery. A neighbouring king of Tutankhamun's said that in Egypt, 'Gold is as plentiful as dust.' Gold was called the 'flesh of the sun', and was a symbol of everlasting life to the Egyptians.

▲ A jewelled vulture, god of Upper Egypt.

Jewellery was made from gold and precious stones found in the desert, including malachite, lapis lazuli and turquoise. Jewellers poured liquid gold into moulds, and worked it into thin sheets and fine wires. Some lost their eyesight chiselling tiny details over charcoal burners. Jewellery often depicted gods. The vulture, above, was god of Upper Egypt. The pectoral, right, shows dung-beetles called 'scarabs'. These symbolised rebirth because they appeared out of dung as if by magic.

▶ A pectoral from the tomb of Tutankhamun.

'All the property of the temples had been doubled, tripled and quadrupled in silver, gold, lapis lazuli, turquoise, every costly stone, royal linen, white linen, fine linen, olive oil, gum … without limit to any good thing.'[4]

◀ This amulet, like the pectoral above, has a scarab as its central image.

15

WALL PAINTINGS

THE FEAST

Women perform a mourning dance as the mummy is dragged on a sledge to the tomb. There, a table is laid with food for the Pharaoh's new life – meat, bread, vegetables, fruit, wine and beer. The mummy is raised up before the feast and the priest tells him: 'Take your seat before these offerings.'

▶ A priestess feasts beneath hieroglyphics, in this tomb painting from over 4,000 years ago.

A priest was employed to keep the tomb stocked with food and drink after the burial. Tutankhamun's mummy did not go hungry. In his tomb were found boxes of roast duck, loaves, cakes, 116 baskets of fruit and forty jars of wine.

The paintings that covered the tomb walls were also designed to help the dead Pharaoh. They included pictures of servants preparing food, which the Egyptians believed could be brought to life by magic spells. These were written in the form of pictures called hieroglyphics.

◀ A priest sprinkles holy water in this painting from the tomb of a mayor of Thebes.

Let there be given unto him offerings of food and an appearance before Osiris, and an abiding home in the Fields of Offerings.

◄ An incredible ceiling from the tomb of Rameses IV.

There are over 700 hieroglyphic characters, and it took a scribe ten years to learn their meaning. Some scribes wrote them on papyrus in a form of shorthand called hieratic. The hieroglyphics on the tomb walls contained spells, prayers and maps to guide the soul on its journey.

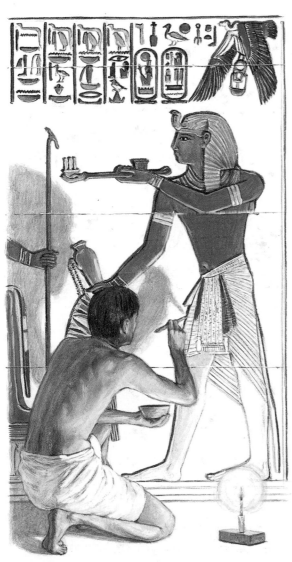

▲ A team of twenty painters drew these hieroglyphics for the tomb of Rameses IV.

◄ A tomb painter using a split reed-stem as a brush to apply his paint.

MUMMIFIED ANIMALS

PRAYING TO ANUBIS

Four priests carry a huge shrine into the burial chamber. It holds the black statue of a jackal, representing Anubis, the jackal-headed god of mummification. The jackal is much feared, as it scavenges graves devouring dead bodies. The Egyptians need their bodies undamaged for the afterlife. So, the priests pray to the jackal, turning it from a scavenger to the god of the dead.

▶ The Pharaoh prays to the jackal god, Anubis.

Pharaoh's palace was home to dogs and cats. When they died, they were mummified and taken into his tomb to keep him company in the afterlife. The priestess Maat-ka-re was buried with a tiny mummy which was believed to be her child. X-rays, though, revealed that the 'child' was in fact a mummified baboon – perhaps her favourite pet.

◀ A mummified jackal or dog, sacred to Anubis.

▶ A mummified baboon.

'Immediately in front of the entrance lay the figure of the jackal god Anubis upon his shrine, swathed in linen cloth, and resting upon a portable sled, and behind this the head of a bull upon a stand – emblems, these, of the underworld.'[5]

◄ The Egyptians mummified huge numbers of cats.

Oh, great Four Apes, seated in front of the boat of the Sun, sending truth to the Universal Lord, extract all the evil out of me.

Many animals were considered sacred. Cats were protected by law, and anyone killing one was put to death. They were buried in cat-shaped coffins in cat cemeteries. Tutankhamun had a pet lion, while Egypt's first woman Pharaoh, Queen Hathshepsut, kept giraffes, cheetahs and exotic birds. Live cows and monkeys were worshipped in temples.

▲ A tomb painting of Anubis.

Mummies of birds, fish, snakes and crocodiles were buried in tombs. At temples, mummified animals were offered to the gods. Some conmen sold mummies for this purpose that were actually bandages filled with twigs and sawdust. Hundreds of thousands of mummified creatures have been found in the underground passages of the Egyptians' sacred animal cemeteries.

THRONE

FUNERAL PROCESSION

A procession of bearers carries gilded furniture into the Pharaoh's tomb. Couches, beds, dazzling jewelled thrones, golden trumpets and a complete chariot are loaded into the chambers. Women wail as the priests bear the Pharaoh's coffin into the tomb, chanting, 'The god is coming!'

▶ A statue from 2500 BC of King Khephren on his throne.

Tutankhamun's tomb was packed with furniture including three couches, an ebony game board and six beds carved with lions. The back of his throne had a picture of inlaid jewels showing Tutankhamun with his queen. One witness called the tomb, 'An impossible scene from a fairy tale.'

▲ This funeral procession was painted on an official's tomb in about 1400 BC.

◄ A chair back carved with royal names, from Tutankhamun's tomb.

These treasures reflected the Egyptian belief that their Pharaoh was a god. Because Tutankhamun was Pharaoh for so short a time, Howard Carter wondered at his wealth:

'If they could bury this unimportant king with so much splendour, whatever must the tomb of a well-established Pharaoh have looked like?'[6]

▼ Tutankhamun's dazzling throne of gold.

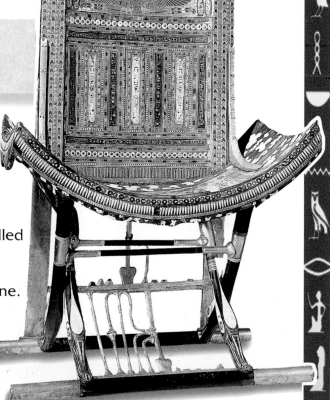

◄ The jewelled back of the Pharaoh's golden throne.

STATUES

THE KING'S SERVANTS

A priest recites the good deeds of the Pharaoh, as the golden shrine of a goddess is carried into the tomb. Other priests write magical inscriptions on to hundreds of small, painted wooden figures dressed like servants. These figures, called shabtis, are loaded into boxes and carried by the Pharaoh's servants into the tomb. The shabtis will be brought to life to become the king's new servants in the next world.

▲ Statues from about 800 BC showing the god Osiris with his son, Horus, and his wife, Isis.

Egyptians believed that they would be asked by Osiris to work in the fields of the next world. They took the shabtis so that ploughing and sowing would not spoil their new life of ease.

'Death is incontestable and we know nothing of what lies beyond. No one returns from beyond the grave to tell us how they are, to tell us what they need or to relieve our hearts until we have also gone there, whither they have gone.'[7]

◄ A statue of Tutankhamun fishing from a papyrus boat.

◄ An Egyptian statuette from about 1400 BC.

Shabti figures tell us a lot about Egyptian agriculture. Pharaoh Seti I had nearly 1,000 shabtis buried in his tomb. Some held hoes, picks, baskets and other tools. Their jobs were to sow seeds, shift sand and water fields. Tutankhamun's shabtis were equipped with 1,866 miniature farming implements. Many shabtis held whips, to make sure that the other shabti workers were not slacking.

The Pharaoh's name was written on the shabtis, which were packed into painted boxes or sometimes miniature mummy cases. Larger boxes, called shrines, contained statues that represented the gods and spirits of the Underworld. These were magical guardians to protect the Pharaoh's soul during its journey through the dangers of the Underworld. Other statues represented the Pharaoh himself.

► This golden shrine contained the statue of a goddess.

ANIMALS

PROTECTING THE MUMMY

The huge, carved head of a cow, covered in gold, is carried into the burial chamber. Then, the bearers lift up the Pharaoh's immense golden shrine. It is decorated with pictures from the Book of the Divine Cow, a myth describing the destruction of mankind. Reciting stories from the myth, they stand the mummy at the entrance to his treasure-filled tomb.

▲ This wall painting shows Tutankhamun welcoming Osiris.

Statues and paintings of animals represented the fantastic gods that would protect the Pharaoh's soul. The golden head shown here, from Tutankhamun's tomb, is of a fierce god called the Devourer, a combination of hippopotamus, crocodile and lion.

The case that contained the mummy was painted with pictures of the gods in animal form. These showed the ram-headed sun god Ra sailing his boat across the sky; the god of love, Hathor, who appeared as a cow; and the sky goddess Nut as a hawk.

◄ The head of the Devourer decorated a couch in Tutankhamun's tomb.

▼ The golden head of a sacred cow.

In a temple in Memphis, a sacred bull called an Apis was kept in luxury and waited on by servants. When the bull died it was mummified with all the ceremony of the Pharaoh's funeral, then buried in a stone sarcophagus weighing over 50,000 kilograms.

'Carter emerged from the tomb ... bearing a grotesque elongated cow ..."What is it – calf, donkey, goat, deer, or rocking horse?" ejaculated the crowd. "It is an Egyptian cow, 3,350 years old," explained Mr.Carter, with a smile. "It has guarded King Tutankhamun throughout his 33 centuries sleep." '8

▼ A fish carved from blue glass.

Fish amulets protected children from drowning. Carvings of the hippopotamus goddess Taweret, or 'The Great One', were kept by pregnant women for protection during childbirth. They were painted with water plant designs representing the hippo's Nile home.

◄ A carved hippo charm.

SARCOPHAGUS

THE OPENING OF THE MOUTH

A priest now performs the Opening of the Mouth ceremony. He touches the mummy's mouth twice with an adze and once with a chisel. Then, he rubs the mummy's face with milk and hugs the bandaged corpse, to welcome back the Pharaoh's soul. The priest believes that the dead man is now able to eat, drink and move. The mummy is carried into the burial chamber and placed in the sarcophagus.

◄ This tool was used in the Opening of the Mouth ceremony.

If a tomb robber managed to break into a Pharaoh's tomb, he still faced a tough task to reach the mummy itself. He first had to find his way through four golden shrines, one inside another, their doors sealed with protective amulets and curses. At the heart of these shrines lay the Pharaoh's massive stone sarcophagus.

The granite lid of Tutankhamun's sarcophagus weighed over 1,250 kilograms. Cheops' sarcophagus was wider than the corridor leading to it, and must have been placed in its chamber while the Great Pyramid was being built.

◄ A priest dressed as Anubis performs the Opening of the Mouth.

◄ One of the three coffins that held the mummy of Tutankhamun.

My corpse is permanent, it will not perish nor be destroyed in this land forever.

Concealed within the sarcophagus were a series of three coffins, each shaped like the mummy they contained. In gold and coloured glass they showed the Pharaoh clutching a sceptre and flail, symbols of his divine kingship. Tutankhamun's magnificent central coffin was made of solid gold, weighing 110 kilograms.

► A tomb robber lifts the mask from the mummy's face.

MUMMY

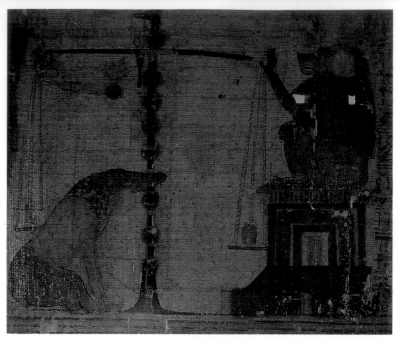

WEIGHING THE HEART

The soul of the mummy travels through the Underworld to the Hall of Osiris, where it must be judged. The Pharaoh's heart is weighed against a feather, the symbol of truth. If the two sides of the scales balance, then the heart is truthful and the dead man may enter paradise. If the heart is heavier than the feather, the dreadful Devourer will snap it up in his crocodile jaws.

▲ The Devourer watches hungrily as Thoth, baboon god of wisdom, weighs the dead man's heart.

The first modern people to discover the ancient Egyptian mummies in their tombs were Arabic. They thought that the sticky resin on the mummy wrappings was a type of oil that they called 'mumiyah'. So, the 'mumiyah' or 'mummies' got their name. People believed that the substance which had preserved the mummies for so long must have healing powers. They began grinding up mummy wrappings and selling the 'magic' powder to put on wounds, or to swallow as a cure for stomach pains.

'The youthful Pharaoh ... ceasing to be the mere shadow of a name, had re-entered, after more than three thousand years, the world of reality and history!'[9]

◄ The embalming process preserved this mummy's head for thousands of years.

◄ This mummy's hand has survived as proof of the Egyptian embalmers' amazing skills.

Oh my heart, speak not against me in the presence of the judges.

By preserving their mummies, the Egyptians also preserved their history. Modern investigations of ancient mummies have revealed evidence of tapeworms, showing that the Egyptians probably drank polluted water. Traces of tobacco – which does not grow in Egypt – have also been found in mummy wrappings. This suggests that the Egyptians may have traded with distant countries from overseas.

Newspapers claimed that the disturbing of Tutankhamun's tomb in 1922 had unleashed the mummy's curse. Two weeks after Lord Carnarvon became one of the first to enter the burial chamber, he died from an infected mosquito bite. When the tomb's treasures were sent to Britain for exhibition in 1972, the Egyptian official who shipped them also died – perhaps another victim of the curse of Tutankhamun.

'The tomb had yielded its secret; the message of the past had reached the present in spite of the weight of time, and the erosion of so many years.'[10]

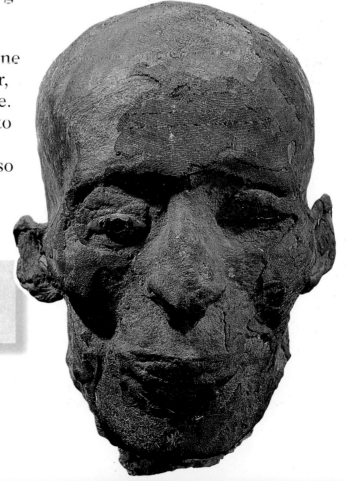

▶ Perhaps this smiling mummy survived the Weighing of the Heart.

GLOSSARY

Adze A tool like an axe with a right-angled blade for shaving wood.

Afterlife Life after death.

Amulet A charm or piece of jewellery supposed to protect the wearer from harm.

Astronomers People who study the planets, stars and universe.

Embalming Treating a dead body to preserve it from decay.

Fertility The ability of animals to produce young, and of plants to produce fruit, in abundance.

Flail A jointed wooden stick used for threshing.

Gilded Covered in gold.

Hieroglyphics Ancient Egyptian writing made up of symbols and pictures.

Immortality Everlasting life.

Myth Traditional tale of supernatural people.

Necropolis An ancient cemetery or graveyard.

Papyrus A reed that grows in Nile swamps, used to make paper.

Pectoral Jewellery worn on the chest.

Resin A kind of gum or glue.

Sarcophagus A large stone box with a heavy lid, enclosing the mummy's coffin.

Scarab A type of dung-beetle.

Sceptre A king's staff.

Shrine A holy place, often a container for the image of a god.

Soul The immortal human spirit.

Stonemasons People who cut, prepare and build with stone.

Symbols Objects representing an idea or quality.

Underworld The world of the dead.

Unguent A soft substance used as an ointment.

FURTHER READING

BOOKS TO READ

Berrill, Margaret *Mummies, Masks and Mourners* (Evans, 2001)

Clare, John D. *I Was There, Pyramids of Ancient Egypt* (Bodley Head, 1991)

Deary, Terry *The Awesome Egyptians* (Scholastic, 1997)

Harris, Nathaniel *Everyday Life in Ancient Egypt* (Sea to Sea Publications, 2005)

Hart, George *Ancient Egypt* (Dorling Kindersley, 2002)

Reeves, Nicholas *The Complete Tutankhamun* (Thames and Hudson, 2007)

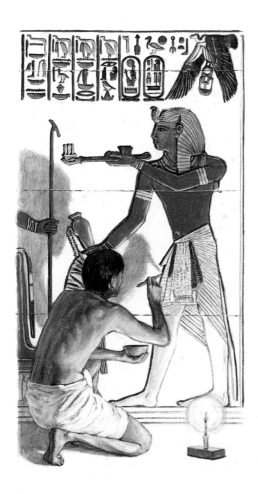

QUOTES FROM THE TOMB

1. An old Arab proverb.

2. Herodotus, *Histories*, 5th Century BC.

3. Egyptian Spells for Mother and Child, in *Life in Ancient Egypt*, Eugen Strouhal.

4. An inscription by Tutankhamun, in *The Pharaohs*, Lionel Casson.

5. Howard Carter describing Tutankhamun's tomb in 1923, in *The Complete Tutankhamun*, Nicholas Reeves.

6. Howard Carter, in *The Complete Tutankhamun*.

7. An ancient Egyptian song.

8. *The Yorkshire Post*, in *The Complete Tutankhamun*.

9. Howard Carter, in *The Complete Tutankhamun*.

10. Howard Carter, in *The Complete Tutankhamun*.

INDEX

Numbers in **bold** refer to pictures.

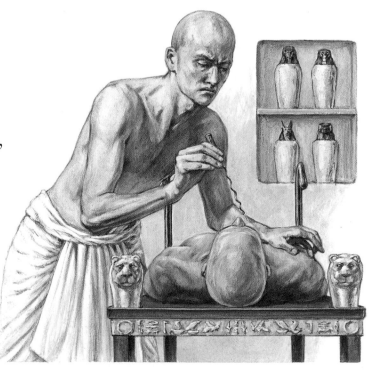